Lively Ghosts
of the
Eastern Panhandle
of West Virginia

by Susan Crites

Butternut Publications
Martinsburg, West Virginia 25401
1991, 1993

i

Published by
Butternut Publications
P.O. Box 1851
Martinsburg, West Virginia 25401

First printing, December 1991
Second printing, June 1993

ISBN 0-681-87306-X

Manufactured in the United States of America

DEDICATION

To those good people of the Eastern Panhandle of West Virginia who came forward to tell their stories, I dedicate this work.

I believe you!

INTRODUCTION

West Virginians can tell a good ghost story. Many times that's because they are telling a story they know to be true. Perhaps, they lived it or they are re-telling something that happened to their Father or their Great-Grandmother.

The Eastern Panhandle of West Virginia is rich in history and replete with historic ghosts rattling and screeching around our most historic towns. It's not surprising that according to the West Virginia Poll conducted by Ryan-McGinn-Samples Research, Inc. of Charleston, West Virginia, released in October 1991, thirty-five percent of those living in the Eastern Panhandle of West Virginia believe in ghosts.

I suspect that there were a great many more ghosts in the Eastern Panhandle that those we learn about in the library or on tours of historic sites. Out of curiosity, I ran an advertisement in the *Buyer's Guides* of Jefferson, Berkeley, and Morgan Counties asking people to share their ghost stores with me.

I was astounded at the response!

For weeks, I traveled throughout the Eastern Panhandle meeting people who wanted to tell me their stories. I met them in sumptuous homes and humble homes. I talked to some in our cities and others who live far from our main roads. Some would only talk to me in a public place where they might not be known. Many lost their nerve altogether.

I was moved by all I heard. Yes, I encountered a nut or two, but most of the good people were earnest. They believed in their experiences, their senses at the time of the event and their memory of its detail. Many offered tangible proof in the form of photographs or video tape or audio tape.

I was given permission to use these stories on the condition that the contributors remain anonymous. I have presented the stores as closely as possible to the way I heard them. I have changed nothing.

There could be many volumes of these stories. I have chosen to share those stores that chilled me with their power and with their obvious truth.

F.C. Bartlett wrote in his book, *Remembering,* "In memory, we find the most complete release from the narrowness of presented time and space."

In this, you will experience the first release of these remarkable, ghostly memories of the Eastern Panhandle of West Virginia.

May those spirits, about whom you come to know in these pages, rest someday in peace.

Susan Crites
Martinsburg, West Virginia

CONTENTS

THE DARKNESS ON THE WALL

Author's Note: As I sat in their dining room, I could see into their large homey kitchen through an opening between the rooms. Children were playing upstairs. Their laughter seemed an odd counterpoint to the earnestness of the conversation we were having. They've lived in Charles Town for more than a decade. He is a plumber, and she works at a local retail store. Their faith in God is the rock upon which they've built their lives. Their faith guided them through the darkest moment of their lives. This is their story.

My husband is a good plumber. He is honest and reliable. We were married right out of high school. We worked, saved our money, and bought this house three years later.

The house wasn't is the best condition when we bought it, but my husband and his brothers had no problem upgrading the electrical system, re-plumbing, plastering and painting it.

The interior of the house had been painted a sickly, dismal green, and there was a big, dark spot in the middle of the dining room wall. The previous owners apologized and gave us a little off their asking price. They said they'd painted the entire house recently, but the spot in the dining room bled through the new paint.

Privately, my husband told me not to worry about the spot. They'd probably used cheap paint, he said.

After the major repairs were completed, the men plastered and they re-painted the inside of the house in cheerful colors we'd chosen for each of the rooms.

About two months later, I noticed that the spot was visible again. We'd been careful to save extra paint for that room because we thought it might need one more coat of paint on the wall with the spot. My husband repainted the wall that night after he got home from work.

You can imagine our shock when we got up the next morning to find the spot on the wall again. This time it was even darker.

Four coats of paint wouldn't cover the spot. I was frustrated, and my husband was angry. He called his brother and asked him if he'd help take down that "so-and-so" wall. He thought it wasn't a load-bearing wall and that a large entrance to the kitchen would be pretty.

That Saturday, they started tearing down the plaster. We all examined the plaster that had been taken from the spot. It was black clear through it. No one could figure out what had caused it. It didn't look like colored plaster or mold or anything we'd ever seen.

When they were tearing down the lathe, my husband called to me. "Come in here," he said. "We've found a treasure box behind the spot!" I ran with excitement into the dining room. I saw my husband and brother-in-law peering at a small metal box. It was about two feet long and nine inches wide. The top and bottom of the box had been sealed in several layers of candle wax.

My husband took a screwdriver and peeled away the layers of wax. We couldn't wait for him to prize off the lid. We honestly thought we might find something valuable in the old box.

I think we all must have seen the tiny skeleton at the same time. It couldn't have been more than ten inches long. There were still pieces of carefully arranged, but rotting, baby clothes on the skeleton. At its feet was a small Bible with a leather cover.

My husband picked up the Bible gently and handed it to me. I held it, and said a prayer for the soul of the tiny child.

When I opened it I read the inscription aloud. It said, "Here lies tiny Sarah. She was conceived in sin. Her new life dooms me to hell." There was no signature and nothing in it told us who may have written those chilling words.

I called our Pastor immediately. We didn't know what to do beyond that. He arrived in a few minutes, saw the tiny skeleton, examined the Bible and began to cry.

"As you know, my Father was Pastor of our parish before me," he said later as we were sitting quietly in our living room. "I recognize the Bible. They were given to children as rewards for verse memorization throughout the Twenties. My Father used to joke about them. It seems a rich parishioner had given the church two thousand of them. My Father said there weren't enough Bible verses or children to use them in a lifetime."

He took a deep breath and said, "This house was built for a member of our parish. She lived here for fifty years or so. She never married and was a matter of great concern to my Father. While she faithfully attended services, she never once took communion or participated in the church in any way. She always sat in the last pew in the back in the shadows. Most folks thought she was crazy."

"The day she died," he continued, "she sent word that my Father should come to this house. He found her in bed, weak and barely able to speak."

"If I can," she whispered to him, "I'll right my wrongs from the hell that awaits me." Soon thereafter, she died.

Our Pastor knew that the old woman had no living relative. Her house had been sold by an attorney for her estate. The money was given to the church.

We prayed over what we should do with the tiny skeleton. In time, we knew that we could right the wrong. The child was buried in a Christian service at a cemetery outside of town. Her marker reads, "Here lies a child known only to God."

Author's Note: They took me to the cemetery and we offered a prayer for the soul of a child murdered by her tortured mother.

5

THE HORSESHOE

Author's Note: I met him at his home near Harpers Ferry. He is a scientist conducting research for a pharmaceutical company in Montgomery County, Maryland. He also holds a commission in the United States Air Force Reserve and returned from service in Saudi Arabia as a hero in Desert Storm. This is his story.

As a scientist, I am predisposed to be skeptical of tales of the supernatural. On the other hand, science explores the unknown mysteries of our universe every day. As our computers and instruments become more and more sophisticated, these mysteries are being solved.

I know of research being conducted by respected scientists into the mysteries surrounding ghosts. Perhaps, science can provide answers to the vexing questions so often raised in connection with ghost sightings. I am hopeful that this latest research effort will bear fruit. While I may be skeptical of the experiences with ghosts reported by others, I know that my own experience was *very* real.

When I was an undergraduate student at Shepherd College, I took advantage of every good

7

weekend to indulge my zest for camping. West Virginia is such beautiful country, and there are so many places to pitch a tent in front of breathtaking scenery, I wanted to experience them all.

One bright, shining fall weekend, two friends and I packed up my '69 Volkswagon bus. We drove to a remote site near Falling Waters and pitched camp near the Potomac. We spent the day exploring the country enjoying the bold colors of the fall landscape.

About five p.m. we hiked back to our camp, built a fire and cooked our evening meal. One of my friends brought a couple of bottles of Boone's Farm Apple Wine which we enjoyed with our campfire stew and biscuits we'd baked in a small, collapsible oven.

I took my old guitar everywhere in those days. As night fell, we put on our heavy jackets, gathered close to the fire and sang every folk song we knew.

About nine o'clock, the exertions of the day, and no doubt the wine, took their toll. We said goodnight, put down our ground covers and unrolled our sleeping bags under the stars. We'd set up a tent large enough to accommodate all three of us, but it often got stuffy in the tent as the night progressed. It didn't seem too cold, and sleeping in the crisp air seemed inviting.

I don't know about the other guys, but I went to sleep within minutes of climbing into my bag.

During the night, I awakened because I heard something. I looked at the luminous dial of my wristwatch and saw that it was 2:00 a.m.

I heard a distant crashing in the bushes when one of my buddies asked softly if anyone else had heard a noise. I told him I thought I'd heard movement in the vegetation to our south.

By this time the other member of our party was awake. He was a forestry major and more savvy about the woods than most. "That noise is to our west, Daniel Boone. It sounds like something is moving toward us. I'm going to get my rifle. You guys stay quiet and still."

"I hear something over there," said my buddy, the art major. "That isn't west, is it?" he asked. "No, it isn't," I whispered. "I hope I'm wrong, but it sounds like we've got something coming at us from three directions."

As we sat waiting for our friend to get back from the bus with his rifle, the sounds multiplied. We could hear crashing all around us. We began to hear new sounds in the muffled distance. When his rifle came into view, I screamed at his sudden appearance.

"Shut up!" he barked. "Follow me. I've found a spot just over the river bank where we can hide. I don't know what's coming at us or why it's coming so slow, but if it's as big as it sounds, we could be in serious trouble if it isn't friendly."

9

We scurried out of the campsite and slid over the edge of the bank. I was so scared, I buried my face in the dirt and curled into a little ball beside my two shaking buddies.

The sounds surrounded us, multiplied, and got louder. I could hear the whinny of a horse and wheels crunching across the forest debris. I began to sweat. My breathing was fast and ragged. I'd never heard anything quite like it.

I nearly fainted when I heard a gruff voice call out. "You boys get back in line. Them horses need room to get by." I could hear men muttering after another voice warned to keep a sharp eye because they were getting close to the crossing.

I heard my friend move toward the lip of the embankment. He moved his head slowly toward the top trying to see what was coming directly at us. As his eyes moved above our hiding place, he cried out, "My God! I don't believe this!"

In terror, I edged up the hill to see what was out there. Just as my eyes focused, several men emerged from the ground fog. They were in uniform, carrying long rifles. Men on horseback became visible. I could smell the acrid odor of gunpowder and the cloying odor of blood.

Steadily, they moved south. There were hundreds of them, tattered and exhausted. They marched toward us and then *through* us. There could be no mistake. This was a remnant of a bloodied Confederate force.

In time, the last of the apparitions walked past. Their noise became distant, and then it was gone. I slumped to the ground. I was drained to emotion, too stunned to speak. I glanced at my watch. It was nearly 4:00 a.m. I realized we'd watched that tragic parade for nearly two hours.

My friends and I walked back to our campsite. A brief glance told us that nothing had been disturbed by the hundreds of men and horses that had surely passed over it. We silently crawled into our sleeping bags and fell into troubled sleep.

The next morning, I was the first one to awaken. My startled cry aroused the others. Everything in our campsite was covered with hoofprints and strange footprints which didn't seem to be either a right or left foot mark. Almost at the same time, we all saw the horseshoe leaning against the rifle case my friend had dropped by our campfire as we fled the site the night before.

Author's Note: He showed me grainy black and white photographs he had taken of the campsite on that morning so long ago. There were prints on the sleeping bags and tent, all around the equipment,

11

even in the campfire ashes. He told me he learned that the notion of a right and left shoe was unknown during the Civil War. All boots were made the same. The horseshoe is resting in a glass case in his computer room.

THE SCREAM

Author's Note: She told me her story over a cup of coffee at Shoney's near Interstate 81 in Martinsburg. She is in her early forties, works as a paralegal for a government agency in Washington, D.C. and bought her home in Martinsburg in 1985. This is what she said.

I'm a no-nonsense person. I do not believe in demons, vampires or UFOs. I don't watch movies about ghosts, monsters or such. Crystal healing, channeling and like can be fun for some, but I think of those things simply as New Age parlor games.

Having said all that, *I swear to you I knew,* almost from the day I bought it, that my home was haunted.

I moved to Martinsburg because it's such a lovely, quiet little town. Since I'd always lived in modern homes, I was intrigued with buying an older home and restoring it. On a sunny day in July, my real estate agent showed me a rambling, Victorian home located between Raleigh Street and Winchester Avenue. I fell in love with its gingerbread exterior and quaint interior styling. I made an offer that day and moved in with my two cats sixty days later.

I was pleased that my home had been built before the turn-of-the-century. I felt sentimental about living in a home with such a wonderful history. Incredibly, I was only its third owner. The previous owner had cared for and maintained the house well. I was eager to begin restoration.

I took a week off work to settle in. I worked feverishly unpacking boxes, arranging furniture, hanging drapes and more for long hours every day. Each night I would fall exhausted into bed with the two cats and drop into a dreamless sleep.

On the third night, sometime after midnight, I was awakened by the growling of one of my cats. As my eyes focused, I could see that both cats were staring intently through the doorway of my bedroom in the hall at the top of the stairs. Their fur was sticking out from their bodies. One was growling menacingly and the other was frozen in his position—too frightened to move.

My first thought was that I might have a prowler outside of my home or a burglar downstairs. I removed the small handgun I keep on my bedside table from its holster, slipped on my robe, and cautiously walked from the bedroom into the hallway. As I left the doorway of the bedroom, both cats shrieked, ran helter-skelter through my legs, and took refuge in the bathtub.

I searched the house thoroughly and found no one. I was shaken by the incident but felt that the cats had simply heard one of the creaks an old house is apt to make. I had a cup of tea and gave the cats some cream. In time, we went back to sleep.

On the last day of my "moving vacation," I undertook the disagreeable task of reconnecting all the electronic equipment I'd accumulated over the years: three television sets, two VCRs, a stereo system with five components, a home computer system, microwave oven, and an assortment of digital clocks. For hours, I labored with instruction manuals, diagrams, wires, connectors, male and female plugs. By late afternoon I was satisfied that everything was working, playing, and cooking as it had in my last home.

Proud of my accomplishment, I called a friend and we went to a local Chinese restaurant for a celebration dinner. I returned to my new home about two hours later and turned the television in the kitchen to a favorite program.

As I settled in my chair, I noticed that the clocks in the television and the microwave were flashing 12:00, no longer displaying the time of day as they had before I left the house. Inwardly, I groaned. Thinking I had done something wrong in setting those frustrating mechanisms, I made a mental note to tackle reprogramming them on the weekend.

In time, I turned off the television and lights on the first floor and walked up the stairs to my bedroom. My cats were on the foot of my bed in tight little balls staring wide-eyed at the top of the stairs. To my dismay, I discovered the digital clocks on my alarm and VCR were also flashing 12:00. I decided that since so many of the digitals were flashing, there must have been a power failure of some sort while I was out that served to deprogram the clocks.

In the weeks that followed, a series of odd things happened while I was away from the house. I never saw anything, yet I would return home to find books tumbled from the bookcases, trash cans overturned, baskets knocked down from high shelves. One day I found every lightbulb in the house loosened in the sockets.

Living with cats, even my distinctly lazy cats, it is always possible that things are moved out of place or overturned during their frantic play. I have known of cats clever enough to manipulate a doorknob to escape captivity but there is no doubt that loosening a lightbulb is well beyond the ability of any cat.

I was growing alarmed. It was clear that these mischievous incidents were not the work of my cats. I was certain something else was happening. I began to jump at every noise. My cats were skittish. We were sleeping poorly. Just before dawn in the second month in my new home, I was awakened by a strange sound. I thought I heard a child's laughter.

"Who's there?" I called.

Again, I heard the laughter, louder and closer. I felt my skin tingle and my heart pound. I was scared. The cats hissed, laying their ears flat on their skulls.

Amid the laughter, I heard the sound of light footsteps moving quickly down the stairs. Then I heard a terrified child's scream. Suddenly, there was a silence so deep and cold and heartbreaking. I shudder as I remember even in the re-telling of it.

In that awful silence I became convinced, in some way I don't understand and can't possibly explain, that I should always leave a light on in my upstairs hallway to illuminate the staircase. From that night, I have kept a light on, and I have never experienced the mischief or heard the sounds again.

Several years after the incident, I met a woman who had known the original owners of my home. I purchased my home from a man who had always lived alone, so I asked her if there had been children in the home of the original owners. She said there were several, as she remembered. In fact, she said it ran in her mind that one had died in the house.

"I think it was the terrible flu epidemic that spread through Berkeley County in 1918 that took one of the children," she speculated.

"No, that's not right," she said and paused.
"Now that I think of it, a little girl broke her
neck and died. That's it! I remember it had something to do with the stairs."

---

*Author's Note: If you want to see this haunted house,
it's the only one in the neighborhood that keeps a
light on all night, every night.*

CALLIE

Author's Note: He was reluctant to talk to me, but he said he had to tell someone who might believe him. I met him and his wife at their home in Morgan County. He is a retired utility company worker, a decorated war veteran and active member of his church. They have three children and one grandchild.

When I came back from the South Pacific, having served as a medic in the Marine Corps, I was eager to put all that behind me and start a good life. I'd saved some money, and my wife had worked as a nurse while I was gone. Our first priority was to buy a nice house in which to start our family.

I'd lived in Morgan County all my life and knew I wanted a house up on this ridge. I knew a few people on the ridge, but a lot had moved to the cities to take good jobs during the war. New folks had moved in, and the word was that some were looking to move back out again. So, I started asking around. A fella at the gas station in Berkeley Springs sent me to see the owner of this house.

I couldn't figure out why he wanted to sell the house. He'd just built it. He said he was tired of West

19

Virginia winters and was selling everything. He was moving his family to Florida.

It was a fine house with three bedrooms, two baths, and a big family room. It sat on eight acres of ridgeland surrounded by dense foliage and large old trees. As he was showing me around the house, I asked him why he hadn't put in a basement or root cellar under the house. "Can't," he said. "There's a great big boulder near as big as the house about three feet down."

His asking price was a lot lower than I imagined, and he said he'd handle the mortgage himself. I could send him the payments direct. When my wife saw the house, she loved it. We signed the papers right there and then! He was packed and moved on down to Florida that same week.

After we settled into the new house, we got busy with our lives. I landed a good job with a utility company, and my wife continued in nursing until the kids came. When we had the youngest boy, the house was getting crowded. I decided to find a way to add another room or two to the house.

One Saturday, my brother-in-law, who was in the construction business, came over to help me plan the addition. I told him about the boulder under the house, and he went out to do some digging. He wanted to see if the boulder would interfere with setting the footers. After a while, he called me from the house. He was leaning on a shovel as he said, "I guess that boulder must be exactly under the house. I've dug three deep holes and haven't hit much more then a rock about the size of a baseball. We won't have any trouble building anywhere you want!"

During the construction of the new rooms, my eight-year-old daughter started having nightmares. She said a lady came into her room every night after everyone in the house had gone to bed. So, we let her keep a light on in her room, and she seemed to settle down.

We finished the addition in November and asked my brother and his wife to come down from Pennsylvania for a visit at Thanksgiving. When they arrived, we put them up in one of the new bedrooms.

That first night of their visit, my sister-in-law came rolling out of that bedroom like she had been shot out of a cannon. She screamed so loud, she woke up the whole clan. She swore there had been a strange woman in their room, sitting in the chair by the bed, just staring at them. After a while, we settled her down. Since she'd been known to take a drink or two, most of us didn't think anything about her wild story. My brother hadn't seen a thing.

One evening shortly after Thanksgiving, I was sitting by myself in the living room reading some business papers when I saw my wife out of the corner of my eye. "What are you doing here?" I asked. "I thought you said you were going over to see your mother this evening." My wife didn't answer. I looked outside and saw that her car was gone. Realizing I was mistaken, I shook my head and went back to my papers.

Not five minutes later, I looked up to see a strange woman standing in the doorway of the kitchen. She was just a little wisp of a thing in a red housedress and looked like she was fifteen, maybe sixteen years old. I remember that she looked so sad and, oddly, I could feel her sadness too—as if it were my own. We just looked at each other for a few moments. Finally, I asked, "Who are you, little lady?" As I spoke that last word, she disappeared.

Over the years, everyone in the household saw her. I don't understand why, but we weren't frightened by her. We knew she was haunting us and didn't tell anyone outside the family for fear that they'd think we were all nuts, but we grew accustomed, even fond of her.

Last year, word came that the man who built the house died down in Melbourne, Florida. The night we heard about his death, I had a strange and emotional dream. I awakened from it, drenched in sweat and crying. When I was fully awake, I knew about our ghost.

Her name was Callie. She fell in love with a man who had a piece of land up here on the ridge. He liked to hunt up here and built a little shack to use when the weather turned bad.

They met at that shack every Saturday when Callie could sneak away from her family. Callie knew it was wrong, but she couldn't help herself. In time, she realized she was pregnant and told him. She didn't know it, but he had a wife and kids down in the valley. He killed her, put her body in an old trunk he brought to the cabin, and buried her. He was worried that her body might be found, so he poured a concrete slab over her body and built this house on top of her. He never told anyone about the murder.

For days after my dream, I drove to every old home on the ridge. Finally, I came upon a weathered farmhouse and asked the old man sitting on a chair under an oak tree in the side yard if anyone had ever lived here named Callie. "Yes," he said, "that was the youngest girl. I'm sad to say she run off with some salesman just after the Big War, and we ain't never heard from her since. I loved that little girl better'n life itself. Nothin's been right since she took off." There were tears in his eyes when he turned his back to me and said, "I believe the missus died of a broken heart over it."

Callie wanted someone to know she hadn't left the family that loved her so dearly. I couldn't hurt the old man any more by telling him what I knew, but after I saw him, Callie left our home.

Author's Note: I drove toward Unger one Sunday morning and followed the road a long way to the ridge. I found the weathered home, and stopped my car. It looked like it had been abandoned for some time. As I walked toward the house, I was filled with a sadness that was not my own.

THE FOG

Author's Note: I talked to several people who told me virtually the same story about incidents which happened in different years, different months, and on different days of the week. In each case, they were in Berkeley County, and it was a dark and foggy night. The following report was given to me by a young, professional couple who frequently visit the Eastern Panhandle of West Virginia. He is an executive in an automobile association, and she is a secretary in the same firm. Their story is almost identical to that given me by a Berkeley County farmworker, a Morgan County homemaker, and by a retired police officer.

I live in Gaithersburg, Maryland and own a small cabin at the Woods Resort in Hedgesville, West Virginia. My wife and I frequently visit our cabin to relax and to escape the pressure of our careers.

Our journey from Gaithersburg takes us up the 270 Corridor to Frederick, then through the picturesque Middletown Valley, and on to a point near Hagerstown, Maryland. We cross the West Virginia border using I-81 and leave the Interstate near the Union 76 Truck Stop. West Virginia Route 901 meanders through gorgeous country for a few miles to the heart of the historic town of Hedgesville. From Hedgesville, we drive toward the Great North Mountain, cross Back Creek and are soon at our cabin in the woods.

As I have said, the drive is through gorgeous country. We always make it a point to make the drive during daylight in order to admire the relaxing scenery.

On only one occasion have we made the trip at night. Given our experience on that trip, I can assure you we'll never attempt it again after dark.

It was late October. The weather was characteristic for that time of year, mild days and cool nights. We'd intended to start our journey to West Virginia at mid-day. Both of us had arranged to take leave from our jobs for the afternoon, but there had been a major traffic accident on 270 just before noon. Radio reports indicated that traffic was not moving northbound and was backed up for miles. I called my wife, and we agreed that it was wise to wait until the traffic was unsnarled before starting our journey.

The accident was one of the worst in many years. We weren't able to leave Gaithersburg until well after 8:00 p.m.

We turned onto West Virginia Route 901 about 9:30. While the Interstate had been easy driving with good visibility, 901 was so foggy in patches that I was forced to stop the car and inch through the fog at no more than five miles an hour. When I came to a break in the fog, I could resume a more normal speed. We must have stopped and started four or five times when I hit the turn by the crumbling Spring Mill Plantation.

Suddenly, it was so frigid I turned on the heater full blast. In that instant, all the windows in the car fogged over. As I rubbed a hole in the mist on the windshield, I saw heavy fog swirling around the car. I couldn't see my headlights, the fog seemed to develop a ghastly, greenish shimmer, and my wife—who is the Rock of Ages—said, "I'm frightened!" Just then, the engine died.

We sat for an instant in the lonely silence. Not two feet from the front of our car a figure emerged from the fog. He was a short man, about five feet, four inches. He had longish, amber hair and a full beard. He wore a grey uniform with a sword sheathed at his side. He was clutching his back with both hands. The hands were bloody. He seemed to notice us. He leaned forward, placing his bloody hands on the hood of our car. He looked at me as if he were pleading for help and crumbled to the ground.

I jumped from the car, leaving my stunned wife staring at the bloody hood of the car. I dashed around the car door to the front of the vehicle. I saw him lying on the ground. I reached out to touch him, to help. As my hand neared him, he disappeared. A moment later, the engine restarted, the headlights came on, and as I walked back to the driver's seat, I noticed the fog had vanished.

I drove the rest of the way to Hedgesville like a maniac. I had to put distance between us and whatever we'd seen. I stopped the car near the intersection of Route 901 and Route 9, pulling the car under a street light. I looked at the hood of the car, expecting to see the bloody handprints. There were none.

I *know* that the soldier who appeared from the fog was real. We both saw him. We both heard the thud of his body as it slumped onto our hood before it struck the ground. We both saw his bloody marks on the hood. Yet, I saw him disappear, and my wife told me on that frantic drive to Hedgesville that she hadn't touched the ignition. The car started by itself.

Author's Note: The Spring Mill Plantation was used by forces of the North and South during the Civil War. It served as a headquarters facility and, undoubtedly, as a safe resting place for the wounded.

LIVELY GHOST MAP
OF THE
EASTERN PANHANDLE
OF WEST VIRGINIA

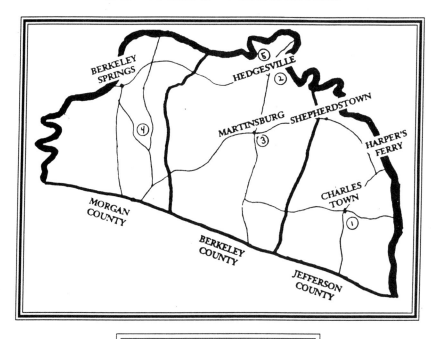

LEGEND
1—*Darkness on the Wall*
2—*The Horseshoe*
3—*The Scream*
4—*Callie*
5—*The Fog*

This appeared in the Berkeley, Jefferson, and Morgan County editions of the *Buyer's Guide,* Martinsburg, WV on Wednesday, September 25, 1991.

Ghosts, Witches Still Can Scare Adults in W.Va.

CHARLESTON (AP) — Nearly half of West Virginia's adults believe demons can get you and a large number believe in ghosts and witches, according to The West Virginia Poll released Monday.

West Virginians enjoy a harmless Halloween prank, but they also still fear snakes, spiders and heights, the poll found.

And 11 percent of West Virginia's adults are still afraid of the dark, the poll found.

The West Virginia Poll interviewed 401 West Virginians by telephone between Sept. 30 and Oct. 2 for The Associated Press, the Charleston Daily Mail and WSAZ-TV of Huntington. It was conducted by Ryan-McGinn-Samples Research Inc. of Charleston.

Asked if it is likely that demons possess people, 43 percent said yes, the poll found.

Most likely to say yes are poor people, 51 percent; women, 50 percent; young adults, 49 percent; and those living in the Northern Panhandle, 48 percent; the poll found.

The poll found that 27 percent believe in ghosts, especially young adults, 45 percent; college dropouts, 36 percent; those living in the Eastern Panhandle, 35 percent; and those living in the Northern Panhandle, 33 percent.

Witches are alive, too, at least in the minds of 22 percent of West Virginians, the poll found. Most likely to believe in witches are young adults, 36 percent; and middle-income people, 34 percent; the poll found.

But West Virginians draw the line at vampires. Only 2 percent admit to believing in them, the poll found.

Martinsburg Journal, September 22, 1991, Martinsburg, WV.

ABOUT THE AUTHOR

Susan Crites, a seventh-generation West Virginian, is the author of several best-selling books set in West Virginia, and has been one of its most popular writers. Her thrilling yet wholesome style continues to earn Crites an enthusiastic national following. She resides in Martinsburg, West Virginia, where she writes about the people and land she loves.

COMING SOON!

MURDER AT CONFEDERATE HEADQUARTERS

by
Susan Crites

When an alert researcher finds a vague reference
to the murder of a junior officer assigned
to a Confederate General's Berkeley County
Headquarters, the Civil War Society launches
an effort to solve the century-old crime.

When they discover that the crime is
remarkably similar to several recent murders in
Berkeley County, they wonder if they have
discovered a killer from another time.

Join Samatha Carter, Denver Casto and the lovable
cat Foghorn, as the most delightful detective team in
West Virginia sets out to solve the mystery
and find a murderer!

Murder at Confederate Headquarters
Another exciting adventure
by West Virginia author
Susan Crites